Pot Luck Rules

ISBN: 978-1-7923-5748-0

Publishing for Authors by Authors!

Chef Kenny's

Pot Luck Rules

Chapters

1. Index

2. History of Pot Luck

3. Reasons to Have a Pot Luck Event

4. Making Safe Food

5. Presenting Pot Luck Meals

6. Donating Money for Pot Luck

7. Using Pre-Made Products

8. Organizing Pot Luck

Chapter 1: The History of Pot Luck and Bibliography

What is pot luck? And why is it so popular? Yourdictionary.com defines as, 1.whatever the family meal happens to be. 2. What ever is available, with little or no choice? 3.

The freedictionary.com defines as, anything that is available or is found by chance, rather than something chosen or planed.

Google dictionary search defines as, 1. Used in reference to a situation in which one must take a chance that whatever is available will prove to be good or acceptable. 2. A meal or party to which each of the guests contributes dish.

Marriam-webster.com defines as. 1a. the regular meal available to a guest for whom no special preparation has been made. B. a communal meal to which people brings food to share usually attributively a potluck supper. 2. what is offered or available in given circumstances or at a given time.

Wikipedia.org defines as; a pot luck is a communal gathering where each guest or group contributes a different, often homemade dish of food to be shared.

Dictionary.com defines as, food that happens to be available without special preparation or purchase.

Vocabulary .com defines as, whatever happens to be available especially when offered to an unexpected guest or when brought by guest and shared by all.

This North American noun describes a particular type of meal, sometimes called a "covered dish-supper" or "dish- to-pass." If someone asks you to come to a potluck or a potluck supper you'll want to be sure you don't arrive empty-handed. The potluck's origin dates to the Great depression of the 1930s-earlier, the word meant "the luck of the pot, of food for an unexpected or uninvited guest.

Chapter 2: Reasons to Have a Pot Luck Event

Pot lucks have been going on for centuries; every country in the world has its version of what is known today in the U.S as potluck.

In the 1930s pot luck in America was necessity for special events do to the shortage of money and resources during the depression era. However people still needed to have a way to celebrate special events in their lives. These events include baby /bridal showers, weddings, funerals, repasts, baptism, bat and bar mitzvahs, conformations, first communion, house warming, and many other family and social gatherings. The pot lucks gave the host a chance to celebrate without the stress and the embarrassment of not being able to host their company due to lack of food or finance.

One thing that all of these events have in common is the social aspect. Pot lucks tend to bring people together, not only as family but as a community.

Chapter 3: Making Safe Food

One of the most important things to consider when making food for any pot luck event is to make safe food. For the average home cook, this might sound foreign, but for those who work in the food service business, this is an absolute must to consider.

Proper Hand-Washing

One of the first things to think about is the proper hand washing technique, which should always be used in food service as well as at home. Wet your hands and arms in warm running water. Apply soap and build up a good lather. Scrub hands thoroughly for 10-15 seconds recommended by the National Restaurant Association ServSafe guidelines cleaning the whole hand including the finger tips, under the nails, in between the fingers and up past the wrist. Rinse hands and arms with warm running water to remove all soap and debris. I personally recommend that this process take aproxmitly 30-35 seconds Remember to dry hands with a disposal paper towel or use an air dryer.

Pets and Pests

Another thing to think about is pest control. If you want to participate in a pot luck, but you have an insect/bug problem (i.e. roach, ant, spider, flies) or a rodent problem (i.e. mice, rat, or squirrel), you probably should purchase some ready to eat foods. You do not want to contaminate food that will be served to other people nor do you want the embarrassment of bugs crawling out of a salad or a hair in the meatballs. You might want to consider either donating money to the host or purchasing products that are ready to use like chips, beverages, cups, plates, or other disposables.

You might not know it, but if you have pets that roam free or shed, they could possibly carry pest such as ticks, mosquitoes, or dust mites. Cats and dogs tend to contaminate the kitchen area, cooking services and equipment. However, if you still insist on preparing foods for your friends and family to partake, you must completely sanitize your cooking space and equipment. You should use warm soap water and sanitize with bleach and cold water.

Thawing and Refrigeration

Another aspect to consider is proper thawing and refrigeration practices. Leaving frozen foods in the kitchen overnight while you go to work is a major no-no. Foods that need to be thawed need to be removed from the freezer and placed in the refrigerator two days prior to cooking in order to thaw properly, or you could place the frozen product in a sizeable container and fully submerge it in cold running water (about 70 degrees Fahrenheit) to allow the product to thaw properly. After the product is thawed, proceed to prepare as necessary. Make sure to clean and sanitize your sink and prep area after thawing and prepping meat, poultry or seafood items.

Dairy

When working with dairy products, be aware of how long you leave the products out of the refrigerator. These foods are potentially hazardous because they are easily susceptible to bacteria growth which causes spoilage. Do not leave dairy products out for longer than 4 hours under 35 degrees. This is called the temperature danger zone. After you've used the dairy product, quickly replace it in the refrigerator.

When presenting dairy at pot luck, it is to be served over ice or with ice packs. You could also serve small amounts at a time to allow the bulk of the product to remain refrigerated. Do not serve products that contain dairy without ice or leave them unrefrigerated for more than 4 hours (i.e. cheesecake, potato salad, cream puffs, quiche, or cake with buttercream or cream cheese icing). Keep in mind how the product will be transported and the distance to the event. Make sure that the products will remain out of the temperature danger zone (41-135 degrees Fahrenheit) for less than 4 hours.

Hot Foods

When bringing a hot dish, it should either be served immediately after cooking within a four hour window, or it should be kept in a heated carrying case (i.e. hot box, cooler, or insulated bag). If the hot dish is to be reheated on site, the maker should cool the dish completely the day before and wrapped tightly then place it in the refrigerator. Reheat the product to a minimum internal temperature of 165 degrees Fahrenheit or better and keep it hot in a chafing dish or Crock Pot to retain heat. Serving safe food, whether you are a professional or a novice foodie, is one of the most important elements of successful pot luck.

Chapter 4: Presenting Pot Luck Meals

Classically speaking, a pot luck dish was served in whatever the guest had available. This resulted in a buffet of mix-matched serving vessels and utensils. Other times, the host had to provide the serving utensils or even some type of platter or warming implement.

Even though pot luck meals are often spontaneous in the sense of not knowing what's in the pot, here are a few guidelines to help you host a pot luck event with a more cohesive, organized, and more appealing display of foods, beverages and desserts.

What to Bring

The first thing to do is consult with the host to tell him/her what you plan to bring to the pot luck. Always ask how many people are attending the event so that you can plan your production and determine what type of serving vessel would better suit your particular dish or dishes. You should ask about the date and time that the food will be served at the event. This information is crucial in determining whether you should transport the dish while it's hot or if you should bring some type of warming equipment.

In the event your dish needs warming equipment, consult with the host to find out if chafing dishes or Crock Pots will be used on the buffet table because there may be limited space due to other guests bringing dishes. If the chafing dishes will allow you to utilize half pans to accommodate two dishes simultaneously in small batches.

There might not be enough outlets available for electrical warming equipment. Remember that hot foods are meant to be served hot and cold foods are meant to be served cold.

If your dishes are served on a platter, remember to arrange the items in a decorative fashion to grasp the attention of the guests. Utilize platters that can support the weight of the food placed upon them. Doubling up on platters will help balance out the weight of the food.

Chapter 5: Pre-Made Products

Everyone was not blest with the gift of cooking or preparing food, but don't let that discouraged you from participating in any pot luck event. **You could choose to donate a financial gift to the host of the event** or bring supplementary items such as decorations, forks knifes and cups. You could also by pre made items.There are wide ranges of quality pre made items from restaurants to grocery stores and small artisan markets where you can perches any number of tasty and in expensive foods from around the globe. Before you perches your goods there are a few things to consider.

- Time of the event- This gives all the participants' time to have all needed products for the venue. It gives everyone the time needed to have everything ready and set in advance.

- Travel time- Travel time is an important factor. This in regards to whether or not the product has to be reheated or cooled before the event. This gives the percipient enough time to safely serve the food.

- Ethnicity of the host- Knowing the ethnicity of the host helps ensure that we can bring foods that would offer a since of familiarity, in terms of cuisine.

- Heating/ Cooling before service- As mentioned in chapter three, heating and cooling are an important factor when it comes to food. Even premade food items must be cooled and heated properly before serving to guest.

- Allergies-Being considerate of each guest allergies is a most. If any of the dishes contain any of the big 8 known food allergens such as, milk products, egg products, soy, wheat/gluten, fish, shellfish, peanuts, and tree nuts (walnuts, pecans) it should be labeled as such, for guest who may or may not know what they are allergic too.

- Special dietary needs of host and attendees- If possible, find out if the host has any dietary needs. This helps in the choosing of each premade item you choose to buy. Dietary needs are not necessarily allergies. For example low sodium, low sugar, low calories, etc.

- Serving vessel and serving utensils- Make sure you communicate with the host ,as to what is needed to serve and plate your dish or product.

Chapter 6: Organizing a Pot Luck

Even through pot lucks can be a spur of the moment event with little to no notice there are a few things that should be considered in order for the event to be successful.

- The venue and the space- If you are expecting more guest then your home can comfortably accommodate you may want to consider the following: Asking a fellow guest with a lager house if the event can be hosted at their home. Next would be to try and rent a bigger venue space, such as a church banquet hall, a hotels banquet or conference hall or if the weather permits move the potluck outside.

- Beginning and ending times of the event-As the host having a beginning time helps you setup and be prepared for the guest and not have to worry about unexpected early guess. Ending time gives the host time to break down or clean up after the event. It also lets the host decompress.

- Who is preparing/bringing what items- It's important as the host to know who is bring what. That way you can have space in the buffet and or room for the items coming in and what is needed to sever them. It also helps with time management. Communication is key. For example, if the person to who is bringing the beverages is running late, it is up to you as the host to make other arrangements for the beverages.

- The style of the event casual, semi casual, elegant, or basic-The style of the food can depend on the theme of the event. For example if the event leans more so to the side of elegant, one might bring lobster bisque, over sloppy Joes. While in a more casual setting one might bring hot dogs over beef wellington. The same can be said when it comes to plating and serving as well as dress etiquette. In a black tie event one normally wouldn't expect to see plastic cups and paper plates, or at a backyard barbeque to see polished china. In a formal setting a suit and tie would be preferred over jeans and athletic wear.
- Set up and break down-When considering the set up of the event, you must keep in mind the set up of your furniture as well as the flow and location of the food. You must also consider if you will have help setting and packing up. In many cases you will move future around, and have lots to move back to its original place and clean.

Dedication

I want to dedicate this book to some very influential indivuals in my life who hav helped shape my culinary career.

Special thanks to my grandmother, Gertrude Ford for giving me my first lessons in cooking. You helped me to develop my love for entertaining and preparing foods for family and friends. Thank you for all of your love and support, I love you!

I will be remised if I did not give honor and respect to my parents Arnold and Bernadette Diggs (A.K.A Mom and Pop). Thank you for allowing me to practice the lessons that I learned from TV cooking shows magazines, cook books, and culinary class. Thank you for supporting my decision on going to culinary school to further my passion for cooking and serving others. Your support is and always has been very important and valuable to my life. Much love and respect Thank you Both!!

To my father, Milton Suggs thank you for your encouragement, love and support. I appreciate your advice a work ethic. I love you Dad.

Special thanks to my mentor, Chef Edward Whitfield for introducing me to the world of international cuisine and professional cooking at Crossland High School. You continue to be a source of wisdom and advice. Thank you Chef.

and allow me to keep pushing the edge of my creativity and artistic boundaries. I love you and I look forward to creating and developing new culinary business ventures with you. Love always your Suggie Bear!

Biography

Kenneth was born in Washington, D.C. and was raised in Anacostia in Washington, D.C. until the age of 13 when he and his family moved to Suitland in Prince George's County Maryland. Kenneth learned how to cook from his maternal grandmother, mother and stepfather raised him. He developed a passion for cooking for family gatherings and special events at an early age.

Kenneth enrolled in the culinary arts program at Crossland High School in the tenth grade which exposed hem to the world of professional cooking, international cooking techniques and dining room service skills. This allowed him to introduce his family to a variety of new dishes.

After Graduating from Crossland Kenneth decided to further his culinary education a the Baltimore International College (Stratford College) where he had the opportunity to study in Ireland to learn European cuisine for three weeks. After completing his studies he received an Associate's Degree in Professional Cooking. Kenneth has worked for some of the finest hotels, restaurants, and catering companies in the Washington, DC Metro area where he honed his culinary and service skills by working with some of the most amazing chefs and front of the house managers in the world.

Kenneth served as a teacher of culinary arts at his alma mater Crossland high School from 2004-2009. He also became an adjunct professor for Prince Georges Community College where served from 2008-2018 teaching several courses such as Introduction to Culinary Arts, Introduction to Baking, International Cuisine, Simplified Gourmet, Fancy Hors d' oeuvre, and Garde Manger and Catering.

Kenneth is the father of two children Dione Smith and Kezmin Suggs who he is very proud of. He is also the loving and devoted husband to his amazing and loyal wife and business partner Chef Nicole Monroe Suggs. Kenneth an his wife have launched a new business venture called Platinum Platters and Garnishes and Monroe Hospitality.

This book is Kenneth's way of sharing some of his years of experience and wisdom with the next generation of culinary students, foodies, home cooks, and professional food service workers.

Ribs Marinade

Yield: 3 Slabs

Jack Daniels Wiskey-2 cups

Yellow Mustard-4 tbsp

Maple Syrup- 1-1/2 cup

Kosher Salt-6-tbs

Italian Seasoning-1 tsp

Ground Black Pepper-1 tsp

Onion Powder- 1 tbsp

Garlic Powder or 3 Cloves chopped Whole Garlic- 2 tbsp

Beef or Pork Ribs- 3 Slabs

Procedure

1. Thoroughly wash all ribs and let drain off any excess water.
2. Combine all ingredients and let marinate for two hours in the refrigerator.
3. Cook as desired, bake ,broil, grill, fry, or sauté

Crab and Spinach Dip

Yield: 10-15 portions

Lump Crab Meat- 1 lb

Old Bay Seasoning- 4 tbsp

Chopped Frozen Spinach- 3 lbs

Parmesan Cheese- ½ cup

Monterey Jack Cheese- ½ cup

Melted Butter- ½ cup

Garlic powder- 1 tbsp

Kosher Salt- ½ tsp

Ground Black Pepper- ½ tsp

Heavy Cream- 1 qt

Cream Cheese- 8 oz

Procedures

1. Combine frozen spinach, crab meat and all other ingredients and mix thoroughly.

2. Place in an oven proof pan, cover and bake until all ingredients have melted and are thoroughly cooked. The internal temperature should be at a minimum of 165 Degrees.

Salmon Marinade

Yield: 8 portions

Salmon Filets, Fresh- (8) 6 oz pieces

Kosher Salt- ½ tsp

Ground Black Pepper- ¼ tsp

Chopped Garlic- 1 tsp

Fresh Chopped Parsley- 1 tsp

Fresh Chopped Dill- 1 tsp

Extra virgin Olive Oil- 1/4 cup

Procedure

1. Wash salmon filets and drain.

2. Combine oil, salt, pepper, garlic, parsley, and dill.

3. Dredge salmon in marinade and cook as desired to a minimum of 141 degrees.

Shrimp Cocktail

Yield: 10 portions

Peeled and Deveined-size 16/20 medium Shrimp-2 lbs

Cold water- 4 cups

Bay leaf- 2 each

Cayenne Pepper- 1 Tbsp

Paprika- 1-1/2 Tbsp

Lemon Cut Wedged and Squeezed- 1 each

Crack Black Pepper- 1 Tbsp

Corse Sea Salt-1 Tbsp

Procedure

1. Bring 4 cups of water up to a boil. Combine all the seasonings/spices and add them to your boiling liquid. Next add your shrimp and allow it to cook.
2. When the shrimp turn pink turn off heat and let rest for 5 minutes. In the cooking liquid.
3. Strain and refrigerate until cool to 41 degrees and serve cold.

Cocktail Sauce

Yield: 20 portions

Ketchup- 5 ¼ cups
Chopped Garlic- 6 Cloves
Horse Radish Puree- 1 cup
Worcestershire Sauce- 2 Tbsp
Fresh Squeezed Lime- 1 each
Fresh Squeezed Lemon- 1 each
Fresh Chopped Parsley- 2 Tbsp
Ground Black Pepper- ½ tsp
Salt- ½ tsp

Procedure

1. Combine all ingredients thoroughly.
2. Taste and refrigerate.

Summer Chicken Salad

Yield: portions

Chicken Breast- 4 to 5 pounds

½ of Small Red Onion Small Diced

½ of Red Bell Pepper Small Diced

½ of Green Bell Pepper Small Diced

½ of Yellow Bell Pepper Small Diced

Celery- 1 cup Small Diced

Mayonnaise- 2 cups

Granulated Garlic- 1 tsp

Kosher Salt- 3 tsp

Ground Black Pepper- ½ tsp

Parsley- 1 tsp

Yellow Mustard- 3 TBS

Olive oil- 2 TBS

Procedure

1. Trim excess fat and remove skin from raw chicken breast, rinse and drain.
2. Coat chicken breast with 1 tsp salt, olive oil, 1 tbsp yellow mustard, and ¼ tsp black pepper.
3. Bake, Grill, or Roast chicken until the internal temperature reaches 165 degrees.
4. Let cool to at least 41 degrees.
5. Cut chicken into ¼ inch diced pieces.
6. Combine all other ingredients together and refrigerate at least one hour before serving.

Summer Chicken Salad

Crab Cakes

Yield: 6 to 8 portions

Large Eggs- 2 each
Mayonnaise- 2 Tbsp
Dijon Mustard- 1 Tbsp
Fresh Chopped Parsley- 1 Tbsp
Fresh Squeezed Lemon Juice- 1 Tbsp
Cracker Meal- 1 ¼ cup
Lump Crab Meat- 1 lb
Canola Oil- 3 Tbsp

Procedure

1. In a bowl combine eggs, crab meat, mayonnaise, mustard, parsley, lemon juice, ¼ tsp salt, a pinch of pepper.
2. Add 1 cup of cracker meal into the crab and egg mixture use reserved cracker meal for dredging crab cake patties.
3. Portion crab cakes to the desired size and coat with the remaining cracker meal.
4. Heat oil in skillet on medium heat. Cook until golden brown on both sides, about 6 to 8 min.

Stir Fry Mix

Beef, Chicken, Shrimp, or Pork (optional)

Yield: 15 to 20 portions

Broccoli Florets- ½ lbs

Carrots-Angle Cut ½ lbs

Yellow Squash Angle Cut - ½ lbs

Zucchini Angle Cut-1/2 lbs

Red Bell Pepper Angle Cut- 1 each

Green Bell Pepper Angle Cut- 1 each

Soy Sauce- 1 cup

Sesame Oil- ¼ cup

Brown Sugar-1/3 cup

Fresh Ground Ginger-1 tsp

Ground Black Pepper-1/2 tsp

Crushed Red pepper-1/2 tsp

Chicken Breast (Boneless Skinless) - 6 each cut into strips

Strip Steaks (3) - 2 pounds

Medium Shrimp -2 pounds

Procedure

1. In a mixing bowl combine sesame oil, brown sugar, ginger, black pepper, and crushed red pepper to make the stir fry marinade.

2. In a hot wok or sauté pan add 1 tbsp of sesame oil and cook 2 oz of the chicken and 2 oz of the beef until well cooked.

3. After the meats are cooked add ¼ cup of each vegetable and ¼ cup of the stir fry marinade. Cook for 1 to 2 min on high heat until all of the ingredients have been fully coated. The vegetables should be al dente.

Stir Fry Mix

Beef, Chicken, Shrimp, or Pork (optional)

Honey Poached Apples

Yield: 6 to 8 portions

Granny Smith Apples-6 each

Water-3 cups

Cinnamon Stick- 1 each

Honey- 16 oz

Lemon juice- 3 oz

Cloves- 3 each

 Butter (Unsalted Butter)-4 oz

Procedure

1. Wash, peel, core and cut apples into 8 equal wedges.
2. Combine water, honey, cinnamon, lemon juice, cloves and apple wedges in a sauce pot.
3. Bring mixture to a boil, and then reduce heat to a simmer.
4. Reduce the mixture by half of the original volume.
5. After reducing liquid turn off heat and stir in the whole butter.
6. Serve apples cold or hot.

Herb Grilled Steak

Choose your cut...Flank Steak, NY Strip, Prime Rib, Filet Mignon, Skirt Steak

Yield: 2-1/2 cups

Chopped Garlic Cloves-6 each

Black Pepper- 2 Tbsp

Kosher Salt- 1 Tbsp

Fresh Basil- 1 Tbsp

Fresh Thyme- 1 Tbsp

Fresh Rosemary- 1 Tbsp

Fresh Oregano- 1 Tbsp

Vegetable Oil- 2 cups

Procedure

1. Combine all ingredients in a food processor and grind for about 2 min.

2. Marinate steaks 30 min before grilling.

3. Grill to the desired doneness.

Pork Chop Marinade

Yield: 4-1/4 cups

Grill, Fry, Sauté, Roast, Broil

Dijon Mustard- 1 cup

Vegetable Oil-2 cups

Italian Seasoning- 1 Tbsp

Salt- 2 Tbsp

Ground Black Pepper- 1 Tbsp

Finely Chopped Fresh Garlic- 6 Cloves

Brown Sugar- 2 cups

Procedure

1. Combine all ingredients thoroughly.
2. Place pork chops in marinade let rest for 2 hours before cooking.
3. Cook to an internal temperature of at least 165 degrees.

Collard Greens

Yield: 25 to 30 portions

Fresh Chopped Collard Greens- 1 case or 24 bunches

White Granulated Sugar- 4 cups

Kosher Salt- 1 cup

Large white onion diced- 2 each

Smoked Turkey Necks-2 lb

Cold Water- 3 gallons

Apple Cider Vinegar- 2 cups

Crushed Red Peppers- 2 Tbsp

Procedure

1. Wash, remove stems, and chop greens into 2 inch pieces.
2. Combine all ingredients in a large stock pot.
3. Bring all ingredients to a boil then reduce heat to medium and let simmer for three hours until greens are tender.

Wild Rice

Yield: 20 portions

Long Grain Rice- 6 cups

Wild Rice- 1 cup

Cold water- 12 cups

Italian Seasoning-1 ½ tbsp

Crushed Red Pepper-1 tsp

Ground Kosher Salt-3 tbsp

Black Pepper- ½ tsp

Garlic powder- 1 Tbsp

Raisins- 1 cup

Cranberries- 1 cup

Diced Celery- 1 cup

Diced Carrots- ½ cup

Olive oil-1/4 cup

Procedure

1. Combine all ingredients in a roasting pan.
2. Mix thoroughly and cover tightly with aluminum foil.
3. Bake at 400 degrease for 25 minutes or until all liquid has evaporated and rice is tender.
4. After 25 minutes remove foil and stir.
5. Serve as desired.

Wild Rice

Seafood Salad

Yield: 15 to 20 portions

Lobster Meat- 1 lb- cooked cooled and diced

Crab Meat- 1 lb- cooked and cooled

Large Shrimp - 1 lb- cooked cooled and diced

Green onion- 2 each -cut on an angle

Red Onion Small Diced- 2 Tbsp

Celery Small, Diced-¼ cup

Red Bell Pepper, Small Diced- ¼ cup

Green Bell Pepper, Small Dice-3 Tbsp

Yellow Bell Pepper, Small Dice-3 Tbsp

Granulated Sugar- 2 Tbsp

Table Salt- ½ tsp

Ground Black Pepper- ¼ tsp

Garlic Cloves fine chopped- 1 tsp

Flat Leaf Parsley finely chopped- 2 Tbsp

Mayonnaise- 2 cups

Procedure

1. Combine mayonnaise, salt, pepper, garlic, and parsley.
2. Gently fold in all of the diced seafood and vegetables.
3. Refrigerate at least 2 hours before serving.

Seafood Salad

Tuna Fish Salad

Yield: 4-5 servings

Can Tuna- (4) 5oz cans drained
Heavy Mayonnaise (Such as Hellman's or Dukes) ¾-1 cup
Small Diced Celery- 2 stalks
Yellow onion- ¼ cup small diced
Old Bay Seasoning-1 Tbsp
Granulated Sugar- 1 Tbsp
Sweet Relish (drained) - 2 Tbsp

Procedure

1. Drain all 4 cans of tuna.
2. Combine all ingredients in to a large mixing bowl.
3. Refrigerate at least 1 hour before serving.

Poached Green Beans

Yield: 20 portions

Fresh Snipped Green Beans- 10 lbs

Kosher salt- ½ cup

Ground Black Pepper-1/8 cup (half of ¼ cup)

Garlic, Chopped- 2 Tbsp

Fresh Diced Tomatoes-3 each

Water- 1 gal

Procedure

1. Add all ingredients to a large stock pot.
2. Bring ingredients to a rolling boil and then reduce the heat to a simmer.
3. Cook for approximately 20 min or until the desired tenderness in reached.
4. Remove from liquid and serve immediately or refrigerate for later use.

Cold Slaw

Yield: 15 to 20 portions

Red Cabbage, Julienne- 1 lb

Green Cabbage, Julienne-1 lb

Julienne Carrots- 2 Cups

Celery, Julienne - 1 cup

White Vinegar- ½ cup

Granulated Sugar- 1 cup

Cracked, Black Pepper- 1 tsp

Salt- 1 1/2 tsp

Mayonnaise- 1 1/2 cups

Finley Chopped Garlic- 2 cloves fresh

Celery Seed- 1 tsp

Procedure

1. Combine all of the ingredients in a large mixing bowl.
2. Mix thoroughly with tongs until all of the ingredients are combined.
3. Refrigerate a minimum of 1 hour before serving.

Pizza Dough

Yield: 5 pound of dough (24- 4oz portions)

All purpose Flour- 3 -1/2 lbs + 4 oz
Yeast- 4 oz
Warm Water- 23 oz
Granulated Sugar- 1- 1/2 oz
Table Salt- 1-1/2 oz
Olive Oil- 3- ¾ oz

Procedure

1. Combine yeast, sugar and water in a bowl. Let set for twenty minutes.
2. Add flour, oil, and salt to your yeast, sugar, and water mixture.
3. On low speed blend the water solution and the flour mixture for 15 min until a smooth dough is formed.
4. Remove from the mixer and place in a lightly oiled bowel and let it rest in a warm place for about 40 min. or until the dough has doubled in size.
5. Remove dough from the bowl and portion to the desired portion size. Shape into round balls and refrigerate until ready to use.

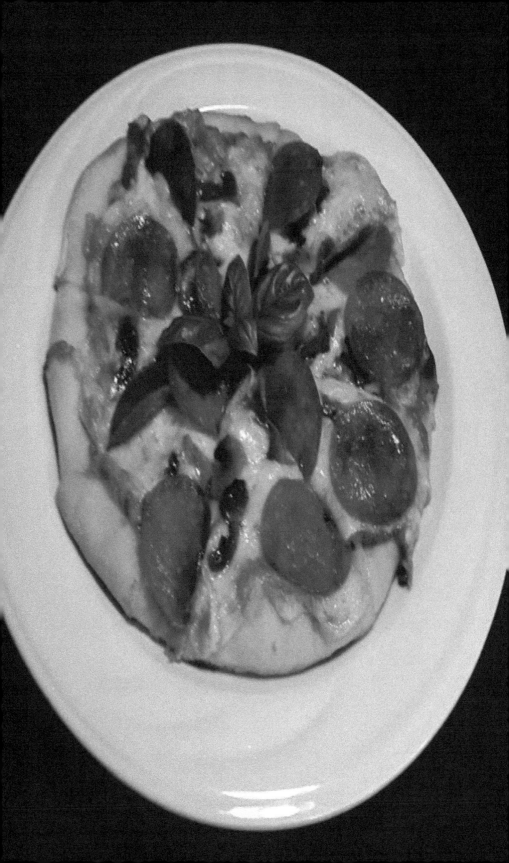

Asian Green Bean Salad

Yield: 15 to 20 portions

Fresh Green Beans-1 lbs blanched and shocked

¼ lbs Carrots- Batonnet

Black Sesame Seeds-1/2 tsp

Ginger, Fresh 1 Tbsp

¼ Red Bell Pepper- Batonnet

¼ Yellow Bell Pepper- Batonnet

White Sesame seeds- ½ tsp

Honey- ¼ cup

Finely Chopped Garlic Cloves- 4 each

Kosher salt- 1 tsp

Ground Black Pepper- ½ tsp

Sesame Oil-2 Tbsp

Soy Sauce- 2 Tbsp

Rice Wine Vinegar- 2 Tbsp

Procedure

1. Blanch and shock the green beans and carrots separately until there al dente.
2. Combine all of the ingredients in a large mixing bowl until well combined.
3. Refrigerate for at least 1 hour before serving.

Asian Green Bean Salad

Orzo Pasta Salad

Yield: 15 portions

Orzo Pasta- 1 lb

Celery- ½ cup- small diced

Carrot- ½ cup small diced

Yellow Bell Pepper- ½ cup small diced

Red Bell Pepper- ½ cup small diced

Red Onion- ¼ cup small diced

Extra Virgin Olive Oil- ¼ cup

White Vinegar- ½ cup

Granulated Sugar- 3 Tbsp

Kosher Salt- ½ tsp

Ground Black Pepper-¼ tsp

Crushed Red Pepper- ¼ tsp

Fresh Grated Ginger Root- 1 tsp

Fresh Grated Garlic- 3 each

Fresh Basil- ½ cup roughly chopped

Fresh Thyme- 1 Tbsp

Procedure

1. Boil the pasta until tender.
2. Shock pasta with cold water.
3. Thoroughly combine all of the ingredients until well mixed.
4. Refrigerate at least 1 hour before serving.

Fresh Salsa

Yield: 15-20 portions

Yellow Onion- 3cups small dice

Red Onion- 3 cups small diced

Medium Beef Steak Tomatoes- 10 each small diced

Fresh Jalapeno Peppers- 4 small diced. (Remove seeds if you want salsa to be mild)

Kosher Salt- 2 tsp

Ground Black Pepper- ½ Tbsp

Green Bell Pepper- 1 cup small diced

Red Bell pepper- 1 cup small diced

Granulated Sugar-1 tsp

Lemon- 1 fresh squeezed

Lime- 1 fresh squeezed

White Wine Vinegar- ¼ cup

Procedure

1. In a large bowl combine all ingredients until mixed thoroughly.
2. Refrigerate one hour before serving.

Potato Salad

Yield: 20 to 25 portions

Potatoes- 10 lbs

Mayonnaise- 2 cups

Mustard- ½ cup

Sweet Relish- 1 cup

Celery- 1 cup small diced

Yellow Onion- 1 cup small diced

Table Salt- 4 tsp

Granulated Sugar- 3 Tbsp

Ground Black Pepper- 2 Tbsp

Green Bell Pepper- 1 cup small diced

Red Bell Pepper- 1 cup small diced

Celery seed- 1 tsp

Crushed Red Peppers- 1 tsp

Procedure

1. Wash, peal if desired, dice, and par boil potatoes.
2. When potatoes are fork tender strain all water.
3. Allow potatoes to cool thoroughly before mixing with other ingredients.
4. In a large container combine all ingredients.
5. Refrigerate at least 2 hours before serving.

Potato Salad

Red Cabbage Salad

Yield: 10 to 15 portions

Red Cabbage- 2 lbs

Red Onion- 1 ½ cup (julienne)

Sesame Oil- 1 tsp

Mayonnaise- 2 cups

Carrots- 2 cups julienne

Garlic Powder- 1 Tbsp

Honey- ¼ cup

Apple Cider Vinegar- 1 cup

Crushed Red Pepper- 1 tsp

Kosher Salt- 1 TBS

Ground Black Pepper- ½ TBS

Procedure

1. Combine all of the ingredients in a large mixing bowl.
2. Be sure that all ingredients are well mixed.
3. Allow the mixture to marinate in the refrigerator for at least 2 hours before serving.

Seafood Pasta Salad
Yield: 15 to 20 portions

Penne Pasta-1 lbs
Cooked lobster tail- 4 oz small diced
Jumbo Lump Crab Meat- 4 oz pasteurized or cooked
(crumbled)
Salad shrimp- 140-150- 4 oz cooked
Canned Tuna- 4 oz crumbed
Mayonnaise- 3 cups
Kosher Salt- ½ tsp
Ground Black Pepper-1/4 tsp
Garlic Powder-1 tsp
White Onion-1/4 cup small diced
Carrots-1/4 cup small diced
Celery-1/4 cup small diced
Green Bell Pepper- ¼ cup small diced
Red Bell Pepper-1/4 cup small dice
Fresh Chopped Basil- 1 TBS
Granulated Sugar-1/2 cup
Rice Wine Vinegar- 1/8 cup

Procedure

1. Boil pasta until tender.
2. Shock with ice water, and drain thoroughly.
3. Combine all ingredients and mix thoroughly.

Spring Salad

Yield: 15-20 portions

Baby Spinach-1/4 lbs

Flat leaf Parsley- 2 bunches

Cilantro- 2 bunches

Basil- ¼ lbs

Baby Bock Choy- 2 each separated and cut in 1inch diced

Arugula- ¼ lbs

Baby Endive- 2 each separated and cut in 1" dice

Shaved Red Onion-1 cup use a mandolin

Shaved Carrots- 4 oz

Cucumber- 4 oz

Radicchio- 1 each separated and cut into 1inch diced

Procedure

1. Rinse all greens, herbs, and vegetables.
2. Separate the stems from the cilantro, parsley, basil and spinach
3. With a mandolin set on the thinnest setting began to shave the onions, carrots, and cucumbers.
4. Cut the Radicchio, endive and Bok Choy in to 1inch pieces.
5. Gently combine all of the ingredients in a large bowl.
6. Cover with several damp paper towels and wrap tightly with plastic wrap and refrigerate for at least 30 min to crisp the greens and allow the cucumber and onion to release its flavor.

Spring Salad

Alfredo Sauce

Yield: 20 2oz portions

Heavy Cream- 2 quarts

Unsalted Butter- 8 oz

All Purpose Flour- 4 oz

 Parmesan Cheese- 2 cups

White Wine- 1 cup

Granulated Garlic Powder- 3 TBS

Chopped Parsley- 2 TBS

White Pepper- 1 TBS

Procedure

1. In a large sauce pan on medium heat melt the butter making sure not to burn the butter.
2. Add the flour and stir to form a paste.
3. Add the white wine and cook for 1 min.
4. Add the heavy cream, salt, and white pepper.
5. Bring to a simmer and add the parmesan cheese, reduce heat to low.
6. Whisk thoroughly until smooth.
7. Use to cover pasts, Chicken, shrimp, crab, or vegetables.

Beef Stroganoff

Yield: 20 to 25 portions

New York Strip Steaks- 2 ½ to 3 pounds

Button Mushrooms- 1 lb sliced

Water- 2 Gallons

Beef Bouillon Cubes- 3 each

Worcestershire Sauce- ½ cup

Salt- 3 Tbsp

Ground Black Pepper- 1 ½ Tbsp

Red Cooking Wine- 2 cups

Heavy Cream- ½ cup

Melted Unsalted Butter- 1 cup

All Purpose flour- 1/2 cup

Procedure

1. Season the steaks with 1 Tbsp salt, ½ Tbsp black pepper.
2. In a large stock pot heat 2 Tbsp of the melted butter.
3. Sear the steaks on both sides about 2 minutes per side until a crust is formed
4. Remove steak and add mushrooms sauté for about 2 min.
5. Remove mushrooms. Add the rest of the melted butter and the flour.
6. Mix butter and flour to form a paste (roux). Let cook about 3 min on medium heat while stirring constantly. Be careful not to burn.
7. Deglaze with red wine and water. Stir with a wire whisk.
8. Add salt, pepper, Worcestershire sauce, and beef bouillon and the cooked mushrooms.
9. Cut the steaks into 1 inch dice pieces and add to the stock pot.
10. Let simmer for 1 hour or until the steaks are tender.
11. After the meat is cooked to the proper doneness add the heavy cream and let simmer for 5 min before serving.

Beef Stroganoff

Fried Fish Breading

Yield: 11 cups

Choose your fish/ seafood: Tilapia, Whiting, Trout, Perch, Flounder, Pollock, Scallops, Shrimp

All Purpose Flour- 6 cups

Ground Panko Bread Crumbs- 4 cups

Ground Black Pepper- ½ Tbsp

Table Salt- 1 tsp

Old Bay seasoning- 8 Tbsp

Garlic Powder- 1 Tbsp

Cornmeal- 1 cup

Water- 4 cups

Procedure

1. Combine black pepper, salt, Old Bay, and Garlic powder. Divide into 3 even portions.
2. Combine bread crumbs, cornmeal and 1 portion of the spice mix.
3. In a separate container mix the flour and 1 portion of the spice mix.
4. In a separate container place 5 pounds of the seafood of your choice and the last portion of the spice mixture.
5. Dredge the fish in the flour first.
6. Next dip in the water.
7. Finally dredge in the bread crumb, and corn meal mixture.
8. Shake off any excess and gently place in hot vegetable oil at 325 degrease. Let cook for about 6-8 min or until the seafood reaches 145 degrees.
9. The Sea food should be golden in color.
10. Store all dry mixes in an air tight container for 5-7 day in the refrigerator.

Fried Fish Breading

Cheese Cake

Cream Cheese- 2-8oz packages

Eggs- 2 each

Granulated Sugar- 1 1/2 cup

Vanilla Extract- 1 Tbsp

All-purpose Flour-4 Tbsp

Procedures

1. Mix sugar and cream cheese in a mixing bowl with an electric mixer. Blend until smooth
2. While mixer is running add one egg at a time until well blended.
3. Scrape down bowl and add the vanilla extract while the mixer is running.
4. With a rubber spatula fold in the flour until well blended.
5. Add to peppered gram cracker crust. Bake on 350 for 45 minutes.

Graham Cracker Crust

Yield: (2) 8" crust

Gram cracker crumbs- 4 cups

Granulated sugar- 2 cups

Melted butter-2 cups

Procedure

1. Combine graham cracker crumbs and sugar in a large mixing bowl.

2. Melt butter and add with the sugar and graham cracker mix.

3. Press mixture in the desired pan, coating all sides.

Salmon Cakes

Makes 10 each

Salmon- (2) 14.5 oz cans

Eggs-2 each

All Purpose flour- 10 Tbsp

Yellow onion- 4Tbsp

Bell Pepper-4 Tbsp

Old Bay Seasoning- ¼ tsp

Salt-1/2 tsp

Black Pepper-1/4 tsp

Garlic Powder-1/2 tsp

Chopped Parsley- 2 Tbsp

Fresh Squeezed Lemon Juice-1 tsp

Vegetable Oil- 8 Tbsp

Procedure

1. In a large mixing bowl combine salmon, eggs, flour, onion, bell peppers, chopped parsley, lemon juice, salt and pepper. Mix thoroughly by hand.
2. Portion into patties and refrigerate for 20 minutes
3. Heat 4 Tbsp of the cooking oil on medium heat.
4. Cook for about 2 1/2 - 3 minutes until golden brown on both sides and the center is 165 degrease.
5. Add more oil to your frying pan as needed.

Salmon Cakes

Seafood Remoulade

Mayonnaise -1 cup

Ketchup- 1 Tbsp

Dijon Mustard- 1 tsp

Lemon Juice- ½ tsp

Cayenne Pepper or Hot Sauce-1 tsp

Salt- 1/4 tsp

Black Pepper- 1/8 tsp

Chopped Parsley- 1 tsp

Dry Dill- 1/8 tsp

Procedure

1. Combine all ingredients in a mixing bowl and combine thoroughly.
2. Refrigerate 30 minutes before serving.

Grilled Shrimp

Large Shrimp- 1pound

Chopped Garlic -1 Tbsp

Salt -1 tsp

Black Pepper- ½ tsp

Crushed Red Pepper-1/4 tsp

Lemon Juice-1/2 tsp

Vegetable Oil- 1 Tbsp

Chopped Parsley- ½ tsp

Procedure

1. Peal and devein shrimp. Rinse with cold water.
2. Combine all ingredients in a large bowl and let marinate for at least 30 minutes before cooking.
3. Cook as desired grilled, poached, sautéed, baked, roasted, or fried.

Garlic Bread

Unsalted Butter- 2 sticks of butter (8oz)

Salt- 1 tsp

Black pepper-1/4 tsp

Dried Basil- ¼ tsp

Dried Thyme- ¼ tsp

Dried Oregano- ¼ tsp

Dried Parsley- ¼ tsp

Fresh Chopped garlic- 2 Tbsp

French, Italian, or any whole loaf bread of choice

Procedure

1. Soften butter.

2. Combine all ingredients except for the bread in a mixing bowl and blend until all of the ingredients are well combined.

3. Slice bread length wise an spread butter mixture on bread. Toast in the oven 350 degrees until desired texture is achieved.

Suggie's Mac & Cheese

Whole Milk- 2 ½ cups
Veggie Stock or broth-1 cup
Melted Butter- 4 Tbsp
All-purpose Flour- 4 Tbsp
White Wine- ½ cup
White pepper-¼ tsp
Salt ¼ tsp
Chopped Garlic-1Tbsp
Shredded Cheddar cheese- 2 cup
Elbow macaroni pasta- 1 lb

Procedure

1. Boil pasta until chewy and drain off liquid.
2. Next melt butter in sauce pan add flour and cook for 2 minutes.
3. Wisk in veggie stock, milk, and white wine. Cook on medium heat for 5 minutes.
4. Reduce heat to simmer and add cheese in small portions while whisking constantly.
5. After all cheese have been added season to taste.
6. Combine sauce with the cooked pasta and place in an oven safe dish and bake for 20 minutes on 350 degrees.

CPSIA information can be obtained
at www.ICGtesting.com
Printed in the USA
BVHW051447220321
603178BV00010B/660